Quick & easy

Dog Training

T.F.H. Publications, Inc.
One TFH Plaza
Third and Union Avenues
Neptune City, NJ 07753

Printed and Bound in China
07 08 09 10 11   9 10 11 12 13

ISBN13 978-0-7938-1002-4

This book has been published with the intent to provide accurate and authoritative information in regard to the subject matter within. While every reasonable precaution has been taken in preparation of this book, the author and publisher expressly disclaim responsibility for any errors, omissions, or adverse effects arising from the use or application of the information contained herein. The techniques and suggestions are used at the reader's discretion and are not to be considered a substitute for veterinary care. If you suspect a medical problem, consult your veterinarian.

The Leader In Responsible Animal Care For Over 50 Years!™

www.tfh.com

Carting and Draft Dogs

In many parts of the world, beasts of burden like horses and oxen were not easy to come by. Therefore, breeds like the Newfoundland, Bouvier des Flandres, Alaskan Malamute, and the Bernese Mountain Dog have been used for thousands of years as cart pullers, sled dogs, and draft dogs. These breeds can still show their inherent talents and strength by participating in sled and carting competitions and draft tests. If your breed is one that historically had this ability and is physically fit, you can contact the breed club in your area to find out more about how to get started training for these events. Once trained, your dog can use these skills not only in organized events, but also in helping you with hauling and yard work.

No matter what you and your dog eventually decide to do, good training will allow you to do it, and you will have the joy of knowing that you are doing it together.

Index

Photo Credits

Table
of Contents

Getting Started

The Right to Be Trained

Dogs not only need basic training—they deserve it. Your dog does not automatically know how she should behave, so she needs rules to follow. Once your dog knows these rules, she is usually perfectly willing to do whatever necessary in order to fit in with the family pack. When you provide this opportunity, you are ensuring that you and your dog will get along beautifully for the duration of your life together.

Why Is Training Important?

When you added a dog to your family, you probably wanted a companion and a friend. You may have wanted a dog to accompany you

Training is an essential part of dog ownership. With proper training, your dog will be a well-behaved addition to your family.

on walks, jog alongside you, or play with your children. Perhaps you wanted to get involved in dog sports or events. To do any of these things, your dog will need training.

Training is important, because it will transform your out-of-control dog into a well-mannered pet that is a joy to be around. A trained dog won't jump up on people, dash out the door, or raid the trashcan.

All dogs need to have someone tell them what to do. They have the right to be trained—it is unfair to leave them to figure out the human world on their own, and they won't be able to do it.

You, too, will benefit from training, because you will learn how to motivate your dog, how to prevent problem behavior, and how to correct mistakes that do happen. Training entails much more than the traditional sit, down, stay, and come commands—it means that you will be teaching your dog how to live in your house. You can set some rules and expect her to follow them.

First, you must decide exactly what you want training to accomplish. You probably want your dog to be calm and well-behaved around people and well-mannered when out in public. Would you like to participate in dog activities and sports? The fun that you can have with your dog is unlimited. Decide what you would like to do and then embark on a training program to achieve those goals.

One option is to find a professional trainer to help you. If you decide to take your dog to a training class, you must do your homework. It should be your mission to find the trainer in your area that would be best for both you and your dog.

Training Methods

Dog trainers are people who train dogs. Dog obedience instructors are people who teach a dog owner how to train his dog. There are thousands of them, and each one will have a method or technique that works best for them. Each method will be based on the trainer's personality, teaching techniques, experience, and philosophy regarding dogs and dog training. Any given method may work wonderfully for one trainer, but fail for another.

Because there are so many different techniques, styles, and methods, choosing a particular instructor may be difficult. It is important to understand some of the different methods so that you can make a reasonable decision.

There are several different training styles. Choose what works best for you.

Compulsive Training

Compulsive training is a correction-based training style that sometimes uses forceful corrections in order to get the dog to behave. It is often used in conjunction with law enforcement. It is rarely the right type of training technique for a dog, and many dog owners do not like compulsive training because they feel that it's too rough.

Inducive Training

Inducive training is exactly the opposite of compulsive training. Instead of being forced to do something, the dog is induced or motivated toward proper behavior. Depending upon the instructor, there are few or no corrections used. Inducive training works very well for most puppies, non-aggressive dogs, and owners who dislike corrections of any kind.

Unfortunately, inducive training is not always the right technique, because intelligent dogs that have dominate personalities will take advantage of the lack of corrections or discipline. They will then set their own rules, which may not be agreeable to you.

In the Middle

The majority of trainers and instructors use a training method that is somewhere in between

If you do not have the time to train your dog, find a professional trainer to do the job.

Quick & Easy Dog Training

Professional Help

Professional dog training organizations:

Association of Pet Dog Trainers (APDT)
150 Executive Center Drive, Box 35
Greenville, SC 29615
1-800-PET-DOGS
www.apdt.com

National Association of Dog Obedience Instructors (NADOI)
Attn: Corresponding Secretary
PMB #369
729 Grapevine Hwy
Hurst, TX 76054-2085
www.nadoi.org

both of these techniques, and inducive methods are used whenever possible. Obviously, the range can be vast, with some trainers leaning more toward corrections, and others using as few as possible.

Finding an Instructor or Trainer

Referrals are probably the best place to start when trying to find an instructor or trainer.

If you have admired a neighbor's well-behaved dog, ask them where they went for training. Call your veterinarian, local pet store, or groomer and ask who they recommend. Make notes about each referral. What did people like and dislike about this trainer? You will want someone with experience so that she can handle any situation that may arise. However, experience alone is not the only qualification. Some people that have been training for years are still using the

Ask the trainer questions before allowing her to work with your dog. Also, request to watch one of her training sessions.

same teaching method and haven't learned any new techniques. Ideally, the trainer you choose should be knowledgeable about your breed of dog, should be familiar with their personalities and temperaments, and should know how to train them. If the trainer doesn't like the breed, go elsewhere.

A good training instructor will belong to a professional training organization. The Association of Pet Dog Trainers (APDT) and the National Association of Dog Obedience Instructors (NADOI) are two of the more prominent groups. Both of these organizations publish regular newsletters to share information, techniques, and new developments with their members. Instructors who belong to these organizations are more likely to be up-to-date on training techniques and styles, as well as information about specific dog breeds.

Once you have a list of referrals for dog trainers in your area, start calling the instructors and asking each one questions, such as:
- How long have you been teaching classes?
- What do you think of my breed of dog?
- What training methods do you use?
- Do you belong to any professional organizations?

- Can I observe your classes? (There should be no reason why you cannot attend someone's class to observe the instructor and the way she teaches. If she says you can't watch, cross her off your list.)

When you go to watch the class, ask yourself these questions:
- Would you let her handle your dog?
- How does she relate to the dogs?
- Are they relaxed and look like they're having a good time?
- Are the dogs paying attention to the instructor?

If you're not sure that you're comfortable, don't be afraid to keep asking questions. You are hiring her to provide a service, and you must be sure that both you and your dog will be comfortable with your decision.

Training Equipment

Leashes

A leash is a very important tool—not only for training, but also for your dog's safety. An unleashed dog can be a danger to herself and to others. A leash will give you the control you need to start working with your dog. There are many types of leashes available, including nylon, cotton, retractable, and chain link. However, many trainers feel that a 6-foot, leather leash is the perfect style to use in training. They are a little more expensive, but well worth the investment.

Will Work for Food

Food can be an important and effective training tool. A treat can be just the right motivation to encourage your dog to sit, come to you, follow you on her leash—almost any behavior is more fun with a treat for a reward. Food also establishes your dominant position over your dog. If you remember to make her sit or wait before placing her bowl down, she will recognize your position as pack leader.

Another useful leash is a 30-foot leash. The length will help you establish control at a distance and can also curb dogs that are inclined to run away. However, be sure to master the obedience commands on the short leash before working with a long leash, because it is easy to become tangled up in the longer one.

Your dog needs to get used to wearing his leash when out in public.

Collars

Your dog should wear a nylon or buckle collar every day, and for training sessions, a flat buckle collar is a good choice. These collars do not rely on pain or aversive training to be effective. When combined with positive reinforcement techniques, the use of a flat buckle collar will achieve results and simultaneously strength the bond between you and your dog.

The collar that you choose should fit your dog's neck

Check your puppy's collar frequently to make sure it is not too tight.

properly—it should not be too tight or too loose. In fact, if you are training a puppy, check his collar frequently to make sure it is not too tight.

Training Area

Ideally, you should pick an area to train your dog that is quiet and free from distractions. Training requires a lot of concentration on your part and your dog's, so don't compete for her attention with your kids, neighbors, other pets, or the television. Also, allow your dog to familiarize herself with the area and explore a bit before you start training. Then she will be able to turn her full attention on your lessons.

Positive Attitude

Always approach each training session with a positive attitude. Praise your dog whenever she does something right and reward her with a treat or with playtime. Before beginning a lesson, always play a little game so that the dog is responsive and "up" so she'll be more

Training sessions should be fun for both dog and owner. Begin and end each lesson on a positive note.

receptive to training. Likewise, always end lessons with play and on a high note, lavishly praising your dog, which will build her confidence and make her look forward to your training sessions.

Quick & Easy Dog Training

Housetraining Your Dog

One of the most important things a dog must learn is housetraining. Housetraining allows your dog to live inside with your family and become a member of the household. Many dogs are given up because their owners claim they can't housetrain them; however, most dogs who are healthy can be housetrained. Don't give up on your dog—by following reliable schedules and rules, she should be housetrained easily.

As with any training procedure, you need to be consistent and firm, and you need to let the dog know when she's doing the right or wrong thing, right away. Timing is key. If you don't correct her in a timely way, the dog won't understand what you're doing and won't be able to connect her act with your correction.

Your dog will not understand the discipline if you correct her for something she did hours or even minutes before. You must catch her in the act for training to work. This is why it is important to watch your dog very carefully when housetraining her. If the dog seems like she has to go out (if she is scratching, circling, sniffing, or squatting) say, "No!" and immediately get her outside. Then praise her for going outside. If you come home to a mess, simply clean it up and wait for an opportunity to show the dog the correct behavior.

Name Calling

Never use your dog's name in a negative way, especially when correcting her. If you do, she may start to associate her name with punishment, and she will not respond to it positively. This is especially important later in training, when you are teaching her basic obedience commands, such as coming when called.

Keys to Housetraining Success
Supervision
When she's inside, you want to confine the dog to a place where her instincts will deter her from eliminating. To do this, confine her to a small area, such as a crate or to a section of the kitchen or bathroom (which has a non-absorbent floor in case of accidents) that you've segmented off with a board or baby gate. This will also serve as her temporary home within your home. She will try to avoid eliminating in her space and fouling where she lives, so she will start holding herself in check more and more as she matures. (Don't put her in a basement or garage, because this isolates her and will make her lonely and miserable.)

Quick and Easy Space Saver

A crate is a very important training tool, and when used properly, can become a second home to your dog. However, that second *home* can take up a lot of space in your *home*, which is why the Nylabone® Fold-Away Pet Carrier® is so useful. It's a new kind of crate/carrier combo that's strong enough for airline travel and, when not in use, folds for easy storage in a closet or under a bed. When you need it, it can be put together in no time.

Confining your dog, particularly to a crate, may seem like a cruel thing to do, but it isn't. A dog will get used to it and even come to regard it as her private place. Many dog owners will keep a crate even when their dog is reliably housetrained but leave the door open so the dog can go back and forth inside it. This allows the dog to have her own special place where she can retreat and get some peace and quiet.

If you use this method of confinement, housetraining your dog will be accomplished very rapidly. Far from being inhumane, it will ensure that you and the dog can live together in harmony for years to come.

Praise

As with other training procedures, praise is very important. When your dog

Praise your dog for eliminating in the proper spot. Kind words and a treat will help to reinforce this behavior.

Hurry Up

There's nothing worse than taking your dog for a walk on a cold, rainy day and waiting a long time for her to eliminate. Some dogs, especially puppies, have a bad habit of thinking that it's time to play when they get outside, and they forget about going to the bathroom. If you start the housetraining process early enough, you can teach your dog to potty on command. When you take your dog outside, use a command for eliminating, such as "potty time," "hurry up," or "do your business." Use any command you are comfortable with and use it every time that you take your dog to the bathroom spot. Soon, she will learn the command and go when you say it.

does eliminate outside, make a big deal of it (and it is a big deal when she's not going in the house). Praise her lavishly, look into her eyes, and tell her how pleased you are with her. It's important to let your tone of voice show that you're happy. Dogs want to please their owners. If she knows that eliminating outside pleases you, she will make an effort to do it again.

Feeding Schedule

In order to housetrain a dog properly, she must be given the same brand of dog food on a regular schedule. If the food doesn't agree with her or she eats too much, it can result in loose stools, diarrhea, or urinating excessively—problems that can defeat the housetraining process before it starts.

Give your dog a brand of food that will enhance her chances of having normal bowel movements. Do not switch the dog's food suddenly, as this is sure to result in stomach upset. Feed a young dog the same brand of food that she had been eating from her previous home. If you wish to change brands, do so gradually, mixing the new food with the old until the dog's stomach is settled. It's important, again, to follow routine: Feed, walk, and water the dog at the same times every day.

A dog must get adequate meals to meet her nutritional needs; however, if you find that she's leaving food in her bowl, it means that she's getting too much food, so you should give her less. If she's going to the bathroom excessively, it may mean the same thing.

As mentioned, a dog's stomach is sensitive, so you should not feed her table scraps during her training period or violate the schedule in any way. Of course, you shouldn't leave food and water on the floor all day. The more she eats and drinks, the greater the likelihood is of her going to the bathroom when she shouldn't.

Outside Schedule

Dogs who are not housetrained should be taken outside often. The more access your dog has to the outside world, the less the chances are that she'll have an accident in the house. If you schedule daily

Setting up a feeding schedule will help you judge when your dog needs to be taken outside to eliminate. Any variation from the schedule that you set may cause your dog to have an accident in the house.

If your dog is not housetrained, she will require a lot of time outside to prevent accidents in the house.

Quick & Easy Dog Training

Ring My Bell

Dogs usually learn very quickly how to get your attention when they want to go out. Unfortunately, they may learn some bad habits in the process—like barking, whining, jumping on you, or scratching at your door. You can redirect this behavior and teach your dog a positive way to get your attention, such as ringing a bell to go outside. Hang a cowbell on the back door and smear it with some kind of treat—a little cheese works well. Each time you take your dog outside to potty, have her reach up to lick off the cheese, thereby ringing the bell. Also ring the bell every time you let your dog out. The action of going out is now associated with the sound of the bell and the treat. After a few months, your dog should get the picture and start ringing the bell to go outside.

outside time and stick to it, you will see your dog progress with housetraining. Every person and family will have a different routine—there is no one right schedule for everyone. Just make sure that you arrange times and duties that everyone can stick with. The schedule you set up will have to work with your normal routine and lifestyle.

Your first priority in the morning will be to get the dog outdoors. Just how early this is will depend more on your dog than on you. Once your dog comes to expect a morning walk, there will be no doubt in your mind when she needs to go out. You will also very quickly learn to tell a dog's "emergency" signals. Do not test the young dog's ability for self-control. A vocal demand to be let out is confirmation that the housetraining lesson is learned.

The following is an example of a schedule that might work for you and your family. Remember that any schedule can work as long as you can give your dog the necessary attention.

7:00 am—Take the dog outside (this time might be even earlier for young puppies who have a hard time holding it all night). After she goes potty, give her lots of praise and bring her back inside. Fix the dog's breakfast, offer water, and then take her out in the backyard again.

8:00 am—Go outside to play with the dog for a few minutes before leaving for the day. Just before you leave, put her inside the crate or confine her to a safe area and give her a treat and a toy.

12:00 pm—If at all possible, come home for lunch, let your dog out of her area or crate, and bring her outside to eliminate. Take this time to exercise and play with your dog. If you or another family member can't do it, try to find a neighbor (a retired person or stay-at-home mom might be a good idea) to come over.

Watch your dog and learn the telltale signs that she needs to be taken outside. Circling and barking can indicate that your dog needs to eliminate.

3:00 pm—If you have school-aged children, make sure one of them comes straight home from school to take the dog outside, walk, and play with her for a while. After playing, let the dog hang out while your child does homework or watches television. If you do not have kids, you may be able to pay a teenager in your neighborhood to come over after school and take the dog for a walk.

6:00 pm—If you are just arriving home and your dog has been confined for a few hours, immediately let

Quick & Easy Dog Training

Accidents will happen. Never yell at or scold your dog unless you catch her in the act.

her outside to eliminate and play. Feed the dog after you eat dinner and take her outside to potty.

8:00 pm—After some quality family time, dog included, do a little bit of grooming, offer some water, and then take her outside to eliminate.

11:00 pm—Take the dog outside one last time before going to bed. If you are using a crate, keep in mind that she should not remain in the crate for longer than three to four hours at a time, except during the night. In addition, the dog will need to go out after waking up, after eating, after playtime, and every three to four hours in between.

Stick To It

When housetraining, don't let success go to your head. A few weeks without a mistake doesn't mean that your dog is completely housetrained; it means your routine is working. Stick to the schedule for as long as possible. A regular schedule will be helpful throughout the dog's lifetime.

Accidents Will Happen

Remember, if the dog has an accident, it means that she was not supervised well enough or wasn't taken outside in time. If you catch your dog in the act, don't yell or scold her. Simply say, "No!" loudly, which should startle and stop the dog. Pick her up and go outside so she can continue eliminating in the regular relief area. Praise the pup for finishing outside. If you scold or punish her, you are teaching her that you think going potty is wrong. Your dog will become sneaky about it, and you will find puddles and piles in strange places. Don't concentrate on correction; emphasize the praise for eliminating in the right place.

If your dog does eliminate in your house, make sure you clean it up right away with a pet-odor neutralizer, which can be bought in a pet store. You can also scrub the area thoroughly with a solution of one-fourth cup of white vinegar and a squirt of liquid detergent mixed with a quart of warm water.

Housetraining is one of the most important gifts we can give our dogs. It allows them to live as one of the family. Mistakes will happen, especially in the beginning. Do not worry—with the proper training and lots of patience, every dog can be housetrained.

Basic Training for Good Behavior

You can begin training your dog as soon as she is comfortable in your home and knows her name. There are two very important things to remember when training: Train in an area without any potential distractions and keep all lessons short. Eliminating any distraction is important because it is essential that you have your dog's full attention. This is not possible if there are other people, other dogs, butterflies, or birds to play with. Also, if you are working with a puppy or younger dog, remember that they have very short attention spans. However, you can give the puppy more than one lesson a day, three being as many as recommended, each spaced well apart. If you train any longer, the dog will become

The come command is the most important one for your dog to master. It may save her life in a dangerous situation.

bored, and you will end the session negatively, which you should never do.

The Come Command

The come command is possibly the most important one you can teach—it may even save your dog's life someday. It ensures that your dog will return to you immediately when you call, even if there is any kind of distraction or danger nearby. Teaching your dog to come when called should always be a pleasant experience. You

Close to You

The easiest time to teach the come command is as soon as you get your dog home. Most dogs feel a little insecure and will want to be near you anyway. Take advantage of this natural reaction. Whenever she decides to run to you, say "Come" and praise her when she reaches you. The dog will learn to associate the action with the words, and it will reinforce your position as the pack leader.

should never call your dog to you in order to scold or yell at her, or else she will soon learn not to respond. When your dog does come to you, make sure to give her lots of praise, petting, and, in the beginning, a treat. If your dog expects happy things when reaching your side, you'll never have trouble getting her to come to you.

Start with your dog on a long lead (about 30 feet in length) and have plenty of treats that she likes in your pocket. The treat should be easy to give and easy for your dog to eat. Slices of hot dog, small bits of cheese, or cooked meat work well; however, don't overfeed! Walk the distance of the lead, then crouch down and say, "Come, Trixie." Make sure that you use a happy, excited tone of voice and use the dog's name. Your dog should come to you enthusiastically. If not, use the long lead to pull her toward you, but continue to use that happy tone of voice. She should learn from the start that ignoring the come command is not an option. Give lots of praise and a treat when your dog reaches your side. Continue to use the long lead until she is consistently obeying your command.

The Sit Command

As with most basic commands, your dog will learn this one in just a few lessons. One 15-minute lesson each day should do the trick. Some trainers will advise you not to proceed to other commands until the previous one has been learned. However, a bright dog is quite capable of handling more than one command per lesson or per

Teaching your dog to sit may take some practice. Take your time to get it just right.

day. As time progresses, you will be going through each command as a matter of routine before a new one is attempted. This is so your dog always starts well and ends a lesson on a high note, having successfully completed a task.

There are two ways to teach the sit command. First, get a treat that your dog really likes and hold it right by her nose, so that all attention is focused on it. Raise the treat above her head and say, "Sit." Usually, she will follow the treat and automatically sit. Give her the treat for being such a good dog and don't forget to praise. After a while, the pup will begin to associate the word "sit" with the action. Most dogs will catch on quickly. Once your dog is sitting reliably with the treat, take it away and just use praise as a reward.

However, there are some dogs that are more stubborn than others, and they may need a little more encouragement to get the picture. If your dog doesn't sit automatically when the treat is over her head, place one hand on her hindquarters and the other under the upper chest. Say, "Sit" in a pleasant voice. At the same time, lightly push down on her rear and push up under the chest until she is sitting. Now give lots of praise and a treat. Repeat this a few times, and your pet will get the idea. Most dogs will also tend to stand up at first, so immediately repeat the exercise.

When your dog understands the command and does it right away, you can slowly move backward so that you are a few feet away. If the dog starts to come to you, simply go back to the original position and start again. Do not attempt to keep the dog in the sit position for too long at first. Even a few seconds is a long time, especially for an impatient, energetic puppy, and you do not want your dog to get bored with lessons even before beginning them.

The Stay Command
This command should follow the sit, but it can be very hard for

some dogs to understand, especially puppies. Remember that your dog wants nothing more than to be at your side, so it will be hard for her to stay in one place while you walk away. You should only expect your pup to perform this command for a few seconds at first, and gradually work up to longer periods of time.

Face the dog and say, "Sit." Now step backward, saying, "Stay." It is also very helpful to use a hand signal for stay—place your hand straight out, palm toward the dog's nose. Let the

The stay command should follow the sit command. Use hand signals to help reinforce this behavior.

dog remain in the position for only a few seconds before saying, "Come" and giving lots of praise and a treat. Once your dog gets the hang of it, repeat the command again, but step farther back. If she gets up and comes to you, simply go back to the original position and start again. As she starts to understand the command, you can move farther and farther back.

Once your dog is staying reliably from a short distance, the next test is to walk away. This will mean that your back is to the dog, which will tempt her to follow you. Keep an eye over your shoulder, and the minute the dog starts to move, spin around, say, "Stay," and start over from the original position.

As the weeks go by, you can increase the length of time your dog is left in the stay position—but two to three minutes is quite long enough for a young dog. If your dog drops into a down position and is clearly more comfortable, there is nothing wrong with it. In the beginning, staying put is good enough!

The Down Command

From your dog's viewpoint, the down command is one of the most difficult to accept. This position is submissive in a wild pack situation. A timid dog will roll over, which is a natural gesture of submission. A bolder pup will want to get up and might back off, not wanting to submit. The dog will feel as though she's about to be punished, which would be the position in a natural environment. Once your dog understands this is not the case and that there are rewards for obeying, she will accept this position.

You may notice that some dogs will sit very quickly, but will respond to the down command more slowly. It is their way of saying that they will obey the command, but under protest.

The down command is usually difficult for most dogs to learn. It is a submissive position in the wild pack situation.

Quick & Easy Dog Training

Down Means Down

Don't confuse your dog by using the down command for anything other than lying down. For example, if you want the dog to get off the couch, use another word, like "Off," to get your point across. This way when you teach the down command, there will be no doubt in your dog's mind what you expect.

There are two ways to teach the down command. With a puppy or a small-sized dog, it will be easier to teach the down if you are kneeling next to her. With dogs that are willing to please, the first method should work: Have your dog sit and hold a treat in front of her nose. When her full attention is on the treat, start to lower the treat slowly to the ground, saying, "Down." The dog should follow the treat with her head. Bring the treat out slowly in front of the pup. If you are really lucky, your dog's legs will slide forward, and she will lie down. Give her the treat and lots of praise for being such a good dog.

For a dog that won't lie down on her own (and most will have trouble doing it), you can try this method: After your dog is sitting and focused on the treat, take her front legs and gently sweep them forward, at the same time saying, "Down." Release the legs and

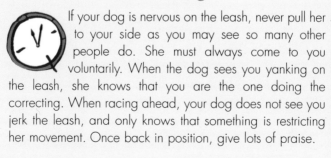

No Pulling!

If your dog is nervous on the leash, never pull her to your side as you may see so many other people do. She must always come to you voluntarily. When the dog sees you yanking on the leash, she knows that you are the one doing the correcting. When racing ahead, your dog does not see you jerk the leash, and only knows that something is restricting her movement. Once back in position, give lots of praise.

If your dog is having problems mastering a command, simply put her in the correct position and give the command. She will soon learn what is expected of her.

quickly apply light pressure on the shoulders with your left hand. Then tell the dog how good she is, give the treat, and make a lot of fuss. Repeat two or three times only in one training session. The pup will learn over a few lessons. Remember that this is a very submissive act on the dog's behalf, so there is no need to rush matters.

The Heel Command

All dogs should be able to walk nicely on a leash without a tug-of-war with their owners. The heel command should follow leash training. Heeling is best done in a place where you have a wall or a fence to one side of you, because it will restrict the dog's movements so that you only have to contend with forward and backward situations. Again, it is better to do the lesson in private and not in a place where there will be many distractions.

The leash you use should be approximately 6 feet long. You can adjust the space between you, the dog, and the wall so that your pet has only a small amount of room to move sideways. It is also very helpful to have a treat in your hand so that your dog will be focused on you and stay by your side.

Hold the leash in your right hand and pass it through your left. As the dog moves ahead and pulls on the leash, stop walking and say, "Heel." Lure the dog back to your side with the treat. When the dog is in this position, praise her and begin walking again. Repeat the whole exercise. Once your dog begins to get the message, you can use your left hand (with the treat inside of it) to pat the side of your knee so that your dog is encouraged to keep close to your side.

When the dog understands the basics, you can mix up the lesson a little to keep her focused. Do an about-turn or turn in the opposite direction. Your dog will be behind you, so you can pat your knee and say, "Heel." As soon as the dog is in the correct position, give lots of praise. She will soon begin to associate certain words with certain actions.

Once the lesson is learned and the dog is heeling reliably, then you can change your pace from a slow walk to a quick one, and she will adjust. The slow walk is always the more difficult for puppies, as they are usually anxious to be on the move. End the lesson when the pup is walking nicely beside you.

Bad Days

If you run into a problem, it is probably because the dog does not understand the command thoroughly, the training sessions are too long, or she is bored. Sometimes, she may just be having a bad day. If she doesn't seem to be into the training session, do a simple exercise your dog knows well and call it a day. Be sure to use praise and play so that you end on a note of accomplishment.

Trick Training

Trick training can be lots of fun, but it all starts with the basics. Before a dog can be trained to do tricks, she must be trained in the basic obedience commands. Being previously trained creates an environment for new training, and in some cases, the basic commands and tricks are related. Tricks are like any training: The keys to success are repetition, timely correction, and lavish praise.

Shake Hands

Have your dog sit in front of you, and when she gives you her full

Once your dog has mastered the basic commands, you may move on to trick training and advanced training.

The Rollover

A fun trick to teach after your dog masters the down is the rollover. Once your dog is in the down position, hold a treat in front of her. When she is focused, bring the treat back and gently help her to roll over on to her stomach, saying "Roll over" as you do it. Complete the circle with the treat in your hands until your dog is back in the down position. It may take some coaxing and a little help at first, but your dog should be rolling over in no time.

attention, say, "Give me your paw" or "Shake hands" and simultaneously tap her right paw and pick it up. The tap and touch will get the dog's attention and focus her to the task, and she should lift her foot reflexively. When she does, praise her.

Repeat the steps a number of times, and as you see the dog is getting better at it, reduce the taps. Eventually, you will get to the point where the dog can do the trick with just the verbal command.

Wave

The success of this trick depends on the dog first having been trained to shake hands. The dog should be sitting facing you. Put out your hand and ask the dog to give you her paw, then put out your hand, palm up. As the dog starts to give you her paw, shake your hand back and forth quickly. Continue to say, "Give me your paw" while the dog continues to wave her paw, trying to make contact with you. When this occurs, say, "Wave" and practice until she can do the trick when you give her the verbal command.

Speak

For this trick, you need a favorite snack as a reward, for example, a square of liver or piece of cheese. Hold the tidbit in your hand and move the treat around as you excitedly say, "Speak." The vast

Sitting up may be difficult for some breeds to perform. Smaller breeds are particularly good at it.

majority of dogs will bark. When she does, give her the treat, praising her at the same time.

Sit Up

This is a trick that also may be too difficult for some dogs to do because of physical limitations. On the other hand, smaller breeds, such as Westies, Bostons, and Scotties, are particularly good at it.

Start by having the dog sit in front of you while on her leash. Begin pulling the dog up with the leash while saying, "Sit up," then drop the leash and stand back. If the dog stays up, praise her highly; if not, repeat the command until the trick is mastered. If necessary, you can also hold her paws up and say, "Stay!"

Tricks can break up regular obedience training and add fun to your routine. They also will make your dog a huge hit with your friends!

Solving Problems

Dogs will be dogs—behaviors that we may consider to be "problems" are often just puppies doing what puppies do. Things like barking, digging, and jumping up are natural instincts to your dog. You must teach her what behavior you want in your home—the dog will not know automatically.

Remember that dogs, especially puppies, have a seemingly unlimited amount of energy and will get into mischief if this energy is not properly directed. Dogs that are bored or restless will look for things to do, such as digging up your flower beds or running out the door when it's opened. If you provide your dog with plenty of play and exercise, she will be too tired to get into trouble.

There are some common behaviors that may cause problems in your house. The good news is that with the proper training and motivation, they can be dealt with easily.

Health Problems

 If your dog displays behavior problems, it may not be because of a lack of training. Some experts feel that 20 percent of all behavior problems are caused by health-related problems. Housetraining accidents could be caused by bladder infections or gastrointestinal upset, and medical problems like thyroid imbalance can cause hyperactivity. Poor nutrition can also be a factor. Chewing on garden plants or wood could indicate that your dog is not getting enough nutrients, and food allergies are often the cause of behavior problems. Before you start training, make sure your dog has been to the veterinarian and has received a clean bill of health. Once health problems have been ruled out, you can start correcting any unwanted behavior.

Barking

Some owners think that they want their dog to bark because they want a watchdog. However, this is a habit that should not be encouraged. Most dogs will bark anyway when a stranger comes to the door or into their territory. What you don't want is a dog that barks at every car that drives by or every leaf that falls into the yard. This is not only annoying to you, but to the entire neighborhood.

Barking can be a problem in some breeds or a bad habit that is acquired. It takes the owner's dedication to stop his or her dog from barking. First, you should figure out the cause. Is the dog seeking attention or does she need to go out? Is it feeding time, is the dog alone, or is it a protective bark? If the barking seems to be caused by something simple, like barking to go outside or to eat, it should be easy to control the behavior.

Overzealous barking is usually a sign that your dog is bored. Keep a supply of toys on hand to keep her busy.

Overzealous barking can be an inherited tendency, but a lot of barking is due to boredom. If your dog barks for attention or when left alone, you can take steps to correct this. If you notice that she barks for attention, you must not reinforce the bad behavior. Never give her attention when she is barking. Wait until the dog is quiet and then use petting and praise. If the barking starts again, walk away and ignore her. She should get the picture soon enough. If you notice that your dog barks when left alone, there are a few things you can try. Before you leave, make sure your dog has been walked, fed, and given water. Be sure to get in some exercise before you leave—a sleeping dog will not be a barking dog. Make sure you curb your dog's boredom by providing her with lots of toys while you're gone. Leave a radio tuned to an easy-listening station for company. Pull the shades or close the curtains. Eventually, your dog will get used to time alone,

Training your dog not to jump up on people is fairly easy. Take a step back from the dog as she jumps up and say "No." After doing this several times, she will learn that this behavior is unacceptable.

especially if she has appropriate outlets for relieving anxiety, like chew toys and a comfortable bed.

Jumping Up

A dog that jumps up is a happy dog. However, while jumping up to greet people is cute when the dog is young and small, few guests appreciate adult dogs jumping on them, especially when your sweet little Great Dane pup continues this habit into adulthood. Your dog needs to know that good manners, such as sitting, are better.

How do you correct the problem? Teach the dog the sit command as soon as she starts to jump up. The sit must be practiced every time she jumps. Don't forget to give lots of praise for good behavior. Remember that the entire family must take part by reinforcing the sit. Each time you allow the dog to jump, you go back a step in training, because your dog will not understand that it is okay to jump on Dad but not okay to jump on Grandma.

Biting

All puppies bite and try to chew on your fingers, toes, arms, etc. Puppyhood is the time to teach them to be gentle. Next time your puppy starts mouthing or biting your fingers, say "No, Easy!" Let the pup know she's hurting you by squealing and acting like you have been seriously hurt. Do not continue to play until she has calmed down. If your dog doesn't respond to the corrections, then a "time out" is needed.

You should be particularly careful with young children, because they can unintentionally play too roughly with puppies that still have their deciduous (baby) teeth. Those teeth are like needles and can leave little scars on youngsters. Be sure to supervise playtime between your children and your dog and intervene with a time out for both parties if the fun gets out of hand.

Puppies often nip at each other while playing; however, do not allow your dog to bite anyone.

A more mature dog should not be allowed to bite—ever. If it does, quickly communicate in no uncertain terms that biting will not be tolerated. A dog bite is serious and should be given immediate

Dogs that are left unattended may become bored and start digging. Keep a watchful eye on your dog and give her lots of attention.

attention. Wash the bite with soap and water and contact your doctor. It is important to know the status of the offender's rabies vaccination. Your dog must know who is boss. If your dog ever bites someone, seek professional help at once, either through your veterinarian, or a reputable, qualified dog trainer.

Digging

Bored dogs release their frustrations through mischievous behaviors such as digging. Dogs shouldn't be left outside unattended for long periods of time, even if they are in a fenced-in yard. Usually the dog is sent to the backyard because the owner cannot tolerate her in the house. The dog feels socially deprived and needs to be included in the owner's life. The dog only wants to develop into the companion that you desired in the first place. Let your dog in the house and allow her to participate in family activities as much as possible.

Born to Run

If dogs are never let off leash except when supervised in a fenced-in yard, they can't do much running away. However, there is always the dog that seems to have been an escape artist in another life and will get out no matter how diligent you are.

Perhaps your dog escapes while you are both playing in the yard and refuses to come when called. You now have a runaway. If your dog is not in immediate danger, the best thing is to use a little reverse

Dog Runs

If you do need to leave your dog outside and do not want your yard to look like a minefield, the best solution is to build a dog run. Fence off a space that will be large enough for your dog to cavort in. Provide shelter, food, and water and keep the area stocked with lots of bones and toys. This way, your dog will get to enjoy time outside without you having to monitor her every move.

If your dog should get loose and run away from you, call her name in a happy tone while giving the come command.

psychology. Do not chase your dog; she will just think that you are playing a game and will run farther. Use what you know, namely that your dog loves to be with you. Try calling her name in a happy, excited tone of voice and then running in the opposite direction. Most likely, your curious dog will want in on the game and start to follow you. You can then turn around and call her to you. Always kneel down when trying to catch the runaway, because a dog can be intimidated by a person standing over her. It is always helpful to have a treat or a favorite toy to help entice the pup to your side.

Remember that when you finally do catch your naughty dog, you must not yell at her. Instead, praise her for coming to you. After all, there could be a repeat performance, and it would be nice if next time your dog would respond to your come command.

Until the dog responds reliably to the come command every time, attach a long line to her collar. She will not be able to judge how long the line is, and you can grab the line without getting too close or step on the line to stop the dog, then just reel in your "fish" with a big smile and lots of praise. As the dog matures and masters basic obedience, she should learn that it is a pleasure to be at your side and should eagerly come every time you call.

Fear

One of the most common problems that dogs experience is fear reactions. Some dogs are more afraid than others—depending on their temperament, the socialization that they have received, and their early environment. Sometimes, dogs can be afraid of a strange object, which can be humorous to watch. They act silly when something is out of place in the house. This problem is called perceptive intelligence. Dogs realize the abnormal within their known environment. They may not react the same way in strange environments, because they do not know what is normal.

A more serious fear is a fear of people. This can result in behavior that includes backing away or hiding, or it can result in an aggressive behavior that may lead to challenging a person or fear biting. This can really be a problem if there are young children in the house who may unintentionally frighten or overwhelm a dog.

Hopefully, you have chosen a dog that has a temperament that fits in with your household. The best type of household for a pup that displays fear or timidity is one with adults that will respect the dog's feelings. If your dog is timid of new situations or people, respect that she wants to be left alone and allow time for her to come forward. If you approach, the cornered dog may resort to snapping. Left alone, the dog may decide to come out voluntarily, which should be rewarded with a treat.

Dogs can be afraid of numerous things, including loud noises and thunderstorms. Invariably, the owner rewards the dog's fearfulness by comforting her. Instead, direct your dog's attention to something else and act perfectly normal. For example, if your dog is barking at the new plant in the living room, simply go up to the plant, touch it, and say something in a happy tone of voice. Don't dwell on the fright. Act normally and show her that there is nothing to be afraid of.

Aggression

Many factors contribute to aggression, including genetics and environment. Improper environments, which may include poor living conditions, lack of socialization, excessive punishment, or being attacked or frightened, can all influence a dog's behavior. Even spoiling a dog and reinforcing pushy and protective behavior may be detrimental. Isolation, lack of human contact, or exposure to frequent teasing by children or adults also can ruin a good dog.

Lack of direction, fear, or confusion can lead to aggressive response from some dogs. Any obedience exercise, such as the sit and down, can redirect the dog's attention and help her overcome fear or confusion. When your dog shows signs of aggression, you should speak calmly (no screaming or hysterics) and firmly giving a command she understands, such as "Sit." As soon as your dog obeys, you have assumed the dominant position. Some dogs may

Some dogs are naturally aggressive while others are trained to be this way. Give your dog lots of love and attention to help control her aggression.

Solving Problems

show too much aggression for their owners to handle. If caution is exercised and professional help is gained early on, most cases can be controlled.

If you have done everything according to the book regarding training and socializing and are still having a behavior problem, don't procrastinate. It is important that the problem gets professional attention before it gets out of hand.

Separation Anxiety

Separation anxiety occurs when a dog feels distress or apprehension while separated from her owners. One mistake that owners make is to set the dog up for their departure. This can lead to barking, crying, whining, and, for dogs that are really anxious, destruction of your house a few minutes after you're gone. The bigger the fuss you make over leaving, the bigger the fuss your dog will make when you leave. Some authorities recommend paying little attention to the pet for at least ten minutes before leaving and for the first ten minutes after you arrive home. If you keep your coming and going as low key as possible, the dog isn't aware that you are leaving and learns to accept it as a normal everyday occurrence.

Quick & Easy Problem Solver

A great way to relieve separation anxiety or just to help keep your dog occupied while you're out is to make sure she has an appropriate outlet. Here's a suggestion. Right before you leave, you can give your dog a ball that dispenses a biscuit when it rolls around, such as the Nylabone® Crazy Ball®. You might also try giving your pet a Rhino® chew toy stuffed with peanut butter or soft cheese. This should keep your dog so busy that she won't even notice that you are gone.

Your dog should not be bothered while she is eating. Constant interference can lead to food guarding.

Food Guarding

If your dog guards her food by growling or snapping at anyone who tries to get close when she's eating, you should correct the problem immediately. First, it is not fair to feed your dog in a busy environment where children or other pets may interfere with her mealtime. This constant interference can be the cause of food guarding. If this is the problem in your house, feed her in the crate where she will not feel threatened. Also, instruct your children not to bother any dog that is eating.

Start by feeding the dog out of your hand, which teaches her that it is okay for you to remove a food bowl or toy and you will return it. Make the dog work for this reward (her dinner) by doing some obedience command such as sit or down before you break out the food. Do the same thing if your dog shows possessiveness over toys. Take them away and then give them back, with lots of praise for being a good dog. This is just another instance of teaching your dog that you are the leader of the pack. Once this is established, there should be no problems.

Solving Problems

Take you pup outside to eliminate before playtime.

Submissive Urination

Submissive urination is not a housetraining problem, but rather a psychological problem. It can occur in all breeds and may be more prevalent in some smaller or toy breeds. Usually it occurs in puppies and may be in response to physical praise or overexcitement. Many dogs outgrow this problem and scolding will only make the problem worse. Try verbal praise instead of physical petting for a while and make sure that your dog has had a chance to urinate outdoors before playing with you.

Fun Things To Do With Your Dog

Once you and your dog have completed basic obedience training, there are many different activities that you can participate in together. Almost all dogs have special skills for which they were originally bred. The trick is to find the perfect match; find the sport that your dog has a natural talent for, enjoys doing, and that you enjoy doing together. Once you find that perfect combination, there is no end to how far you and your dog can go.

Not all dog sports have to be organized events—your dog will be happy to join you and your family in almost any activity. Dogs thrive on exercise and will be happy to accompany you jogging, walking, or bicycling. Some breeds, like Newfoundlands and retrievers, make exceptional swimmers and can be trained for water rescue. Others will enjoy camping, backpacking, and hiking—whatever recreation you are interested in, there is a dog that can do it.

Growing Puppies

If you have a puppy, it is important to remember that very young puppies are still growing; their bones are still soft and they may not be fully developed until they are a year old or more. Hold off on any serious workouts until your puppy has matured physically as it may cause permanent damage.

As with any form of exercise, make sure your dog is warmed up first and builds stamina slowly. Of course, you can't expect a Chihuahua to accompany you on a ten-mile run, so also take into consideration any such physical limitations. Hopefully, you have chosen your dog with this in mind. If you take the proper precautions, your dog can be in the best physical shape like any conditioned athlete, and you will have a great workout companion.

The Canine Good Citizen® Test

A good way to make sure that your dog has good manners is to train her for the Canine Good Citizen® Test. The American Kennel Club (AKC) has developed this program to encourage all owners to properly train their dog. It emphasizes responsible dog ownership and teaches your dog good manners in the home and the community. All dogs of any age, purebred or mixed breed, can take the Canine Good Citizen® Test and earn a certificate from the AKC, as well as add the CGC® to their name.

The dog must complete ten steps in order to pass. These exercises show that the dog is a pet that any person would like to own, that

Training your dog for the Canine Good Citizen® Test will ensure that she has good manners and will be welcomed anywhere.

she is safe with children, and that she would be welcomed as a neighbor. An increasing number of states have now passed Canine Good Citizen® legislation and the CGC® program has been adopted in several other countries.

The AKC encourages all dog owners to participate in this program, and you can find out where a test is being given in your area by contacting your local breed club or the AKC directly at www.akc.org.

Therapy Dogs

There is nothing more rewarding than seeing someone else get as much happiness and delight out of your dog as you do, and there are some dogs that just seem to love getting a smile out of anyone and everyone. Getting involved with therapy work is a wonderful way to spread the joy of dog ownership to those who may benefit

Your dog can be trained to be a therapy dog.

most from it. Statistics show that this is creating some remarkable results with the sick, the elderly, and people with special needs. If your dog has a particularly even and friendly temperament, therapy work may be perfect for her and especially rewarding for you.

You and your dog can visit the elderly in nursing homes or patients in hospitals, or enroll in a program to educate children about the care and training of dogs. Your local humane society can inform you of programs in your area and the best way to get started. A therapy dog makes a valuable contribution to the quality of life of others.

Assistance Dogs

Some dogs can be trained to assist people with physical disabilities. They can help the blind get around independently, help the deaf notice the telephone or the doorbell, and help those confined to wheelchairs accomplish everyday activities like opening doors or getting items they need. There are special programs that screen and train these dogs, as well as foster programs for people who can take in puppies to train and socialize them until they are ready to be placed with that special person.

Search and Rescue Dogs

In almost any city, you will find a canine search and rescue unit. These dedicated handlers and their dogs go to scenes of disasters to help find survivors and victims. They also help find people who may be lost. These handler/dog teams travel great distances and give up much of their time and energy to help others. They do this for the personal sense of satisfaction that they receive, not for money or glory.

It takes a special dog and owner to devote so much of themselves to helping others. Search and rescue dogs come in all different breeds, but all have a few traits in common: athleticism, tracking ability, and perseverance. Getting your dog certified as a search and rescue dog is not easy. You must go through rigorous training exercises under the same conditions that the dog will be facing before you are allowed to actually go to work. The best way to get started is to contact your local law enforcement agency or one of the national associations to see if there are any units in your area. The next time disaster

An assistance dog helps his owner with everyday tasks, such as opening doors and getting items.

strikes, you and your dog could be helping others—and there is no greater reward of dog ownership.

Conformation

Everyone thinks that they have a good-looking dog. If your pet is an AKC-registered purebred and is six months of age or older, you may want to jump into the world of dog showing. In conformation, the main consideration is overall appearance and structure and how closely the dog conforms to the official standard of perfection for the breed.

If you would like to get involved in showing, the first thing you should do is go to dog shows in your area without your dog. Spend the day watching not only your breed's judging, but other judgings as well. Judges examine the dogs and place them according to how close each one compares with the ideal dog as described in the

Your dog needs to look its very best at a conformation show.

breed's official standard. These judges are experts in the breeds they are judging. They examine each dog with their hands to see if the teeth, muscles, bones, and coat texture match the standard. They examine each dog in profile for general balance and watch each dog move to see how all these features fit together.

There are three types of conformation shows: specialty, group, and all-breed. Specialty shows are limited to a specific breed. Group shows are limited to dogs from one of the seven groups; for example, the All-Terrier Show. All-breed shows are open to the over 140 breeds recognized by the AKC. Most dogs at conformation shows are competing for points toward a championship. It takes 15 points, including 2 major wins (3, 4, or 5 points) under at least three different judges to become an AKC Champion of Record, which is indicated by a Ch. before the dog's name.

Dog showing can be a very rewarding experience. But be careful— once bitten by the show bug, many people get addicted!

Junior Showmanship

If you have children that are interested in training and competing, you may want to get involved in junior showmanship. Junior showmanship evolved as part of the concept that dog shows should be a family sport as well as entertainment. It was started in the 1930s and has continually grown in participation. It is now an integral part of almost every dog show held in the US and other countries. It is a great way to teach children how to handle, care for, and respect their pets, and also gives them a good start in the sport of dog showing. Participating in junior showmanship deepens the unique relationship between children and their dogs.

Obedience

You may find that your dog aced puppy kindergarten and loves to work with you practicing basic commands. If you have a "workaholic" on your hands, obedience may be the right event for you.

Obedience trials test your dog's ability to perform a particular set of exercises. The handler and dog team is scored on performance. In each exercise, you must score more than 50 percent of the possible points (ranging from 20 to 40) and get a total score of at least 170 out of a possible 200. Each time you do this, your dog gets a "leg" toward a title. Three legs under three different judges and your dog earns an obedience title.

Hide and Seek

A good way to get your dog started in tracking is to play hide and seek in the house. Begin with a certain toy that your dog likes, such as a ball. First, hide the ball, but let the dog see where you put it. Then say, "Find it." After the dog gets the hang of it, put her in another room while you hide the object. You can make the game increasingly difficult by using different objects. If your pet enjoys playing hide and seek, you probably have a natural tracking dog on your hands.

Tracking

All dogs love to use their noses; they use them to communicate with people and other dogs every day. Tracking trials allow dogs to demonstrate their natural ability to recognize and follow scent. This vigorous outdoor activity is especially great for canine athletes that have an affinity for tracking, such as some dogs in the Hound Group. Unlike obedience, your dog only has to pass one tracking test in order to earn this title.

Agility

One of the fastest growing, most popular, and fun events is agility. It was developed and introduced in 1978 in England by John Varley and Peter Meanwell as an entertaining diversion between judgings at dog shows, but was officially recognized as a sport by the AKC in

Agility tests your dog's ability to be led over a series of obstacles through verbal commands and hand signals.

the early 1980s. Agility is an exciting sport in which you guide your dog off lead using verbal commands and hand signals over a series of obstacles on a timed course.

Agility trial titles are Novice Agility Dog (NAD), Open Agility Dog (OAD), Agility Dog Excellent (ADX), and Master Agility Excellent (MAX). In order to acquire an agility title, your dog must earn three qualifying scores in each class under two different judges. The MAX title is awarded after the dog earns ten qualifying scores in the Agility Excellent Class.

The only problem with training your puppy to compete in agility is finding the equipment and space to train. Many agility clubs can provide information on getting started toward an agility title. Even if you don't compete, just training for agility can be lots of fun for both you and your dog.

Flyball

Do you have an athletic, active dog with a special affinity for tennis balls? If so, flyball may be the right sport for you. Flyball is a relay race between two teams, each with four dogs and four handlers. Each dog takes a turn running over a course with four jumps and a flyball box at the end of the course. The dog presses a pedal on the front of a flyball box. This releases a throwing arm that sends a tennis ball up in the air. The dog catches the ball and runs back over the course to the starting line. Then the next dog runs. The first team to have all four dogs successfully complete the course is the winner. It is an exciting sport, and you may find that it allows your puppy to turn her abilities into a pastime that's fun for all involved.

Flying Disc

Some dogs just love to play with a Frisbee™; they sleep with it, eat with it, and live to play the next game of fetch. Now there are Frisbee-throwing competitions that allow dogs to display their

If your dog has strong retrieving and tracking skills, she might excel at Frisbee™ competitions.

amazing athletic aptitude. It all started in the mid-1970s when Alex Stein ran out on the field in the middle of a Dodgers baseball game and performed with his dog, Ashley Whippet. A nationwide audience got to enjoy the high-flying demonstration on television, and the sport of canine flying disc competition was born.

Both mixed breed and purebred dogs can compete, but dogs that excel in flying disc are the medium-sized, lean, agile dogs that are able to take flying leaps and use their

Quick & Easy Dog Training

Earthdog trials are great for the "go-to-ground" breeds that were originally bred to go into dens after prey.

owners as launching pads. Other characteristics that make a good flying disc dog are strong retrieving and tracking instincts, an even temperament, and sound hips.

Freestyle Dancing

If you enjoy dancing, maybe your perfect dance partner isn't another human, but your four-footed companion. Freestyle allows you to dance with your dog and have fun.

Freestyle is a relatively new sport that began in the 1990s. Any dog, purebred or mixed breed, may participate in freestyle competitions. You can have multiple dogs and partners or you may dance with just one dog. Creativity is paramount in freestyle dancing, and many organizations hold competitions.

Earthdog Trials

Does your terrier or Dachshund love to dig holes and chase rabbits in your backyard? If so, you may have a natural candidate for Earthdog trials. Earthdog trials are for the "go-to-ground" breeds (the smaller terriers and Dachshunds) that were originally bred to

Fun Things To Do With Your Dog 59

go into dens and tunnels after prey, which consisted of all types of small vermin from rats to badgers. There are four class levels at a licensed trial: Introduction to Quarry (for beginning handlers and dogs), Junior Earthdog, Senior Earthdog, and Master Earthdog. The object of the test is to give your dog an opportunity to display the ability to follow game and to "work" the quarry. The "work" is showing interest in the game by barking, digging, and scratching. The quarry can either be two adult rats, which must be caged to be protected from the dogs, or artificial quarry that is located behind a barrier, properly scented, and capable of movement.

Field Events

The American Kennel Club runs field trials and hunt tests that are open to pointing breeds, retrievers, spaniels, Basset Hounds, Beagles, and Dachshunds over the age of six months and registered with the AKC. Individual clubs sponsor these events under AKC sanction or license. If you own any of the eligible breeds, it is quite a thrill to see your puppy develop and demonstrate those natural instincts.

Field trials test a dog's ability to retrieve and flush game in the field.

Herding trials are ideal for those breeds of dog that can control livestock.

In hunt tests, the dog's ability to perform is judged against a standard of perfection established by AKC regulations. Dogs that receive qualifying scores at a number of tests achieve titles of JH (Junior Hunter), SH (Senior Hunter), and MH (Master Hunter), each successively requiring more skill.

In field trials, dogs compete against each other for placements and points toward field championships. Successful dogs earn a FC (Field Champion) title in front of their names. The field events are divided by subgroups of dogs and are sometimes limited to specific breeds.

Herding Trials

If your breed of dog is in the Herding Group (or is a Samoyed or Rottweiler), you may have noticed her circling or "rounding up" bicycles, birds, or even your children. This inherent ability to control livestock can be put to good use by participating in herding tests and/or trials. Herding trials are designed to allow your dog to demonstrate the ability to herd under the direction of a handler.

In herding trials, your dog will be judged against a set of standards and can earn advanced titles and championships by competing against other dogs for placements. Livestock used at the trials include sheep, cattle, ducks, or goats. The titles offered are HS (Herding Started), HI (Herding Intermediate), and HX (Herding Excellent). Upon the completion of an HX, a Herding Championship may be earned after accumulating 15 championship points. There are also noncompetitive herding clinics and instinct tests given by AKC clubs across the country.

Lure Coursing

There is nothing more exciting than seeing your dog do what it was bred to do, especially if that dog is a sighthound racing at full speed. Lure coursing is an event in which dogs follow an artificial lure around a course on an open field. They are scored on speed, enthusiasm, agility, endurance, and their ability to follow the lure. The eligible breeds are: Whippet, Basenji, Greyhound, Afghan Hound, Borzoi, Ibizan Hound, Pharaoh Hound, Irish Wolfhound, Scottish Deerhound, Saluki, and Rhodesian Ridgeback.

Some breeds excel at carting. Once trained properly, your dog can help you with hauling and yard work.

Quick & Easy Dog Training